IN THIS ISSUE

LETTER FROM THE EDITOR

As Editor-in-Chief, I am pleased to present this comprehensive study of Max James, a figure whose name has become synonymous with entrepreneurial excellence and resilience. In this issue, readers will find more than just an entrepreneurial success story; they will learn about a man whose life's work goes far beyond industry awards and financial success.

James' journey from humble beginnings to "King of the Kiosks" is interwoven with invaluable lessons about resilience, adaptability, integrity, and the importance of mentorship. Whether you're an established entrepreneur, an aspiring leader, or simply looking for inspiration, the insights of Max James's experiences are a guide that transcends the realm of business and speaks to the philosophy of living a meaningful life.

Dive in and discover the wisdom and practices of a man whose legacy continues to shape the landscape of entrepreneurship.

Also in this issue, you will find a new monthly column, the "Real Estate Deal of the Month" by Alex Jarbo. Alex is an accomplished real estate mogul, and a veteran of the Marine Corps, who regularly has exciting deals for successful entrepreneurs to invest in.

We are also excited to present two reprints of book chapters from Mike Steward and Mike Jackson from the international bestseller, *Business Leadership and Community*.

Chris O'Byrne

PIVOT Magazine

Founder and President
Jason Miller

Editor-in-Chief
Chris O'Byrne

Design
JETLAUNCH.net

Advertising
Chris O'Byrne

Webmaster
Joel Phillips

Editor
Laura West

Cover Design
Brad Szollose

Copyright © 2023 PIVOT

ISBN: 979-8-89079-033-0

MESSAGE FROM THE PRESIDENT

JASON MILLER

The journey of an entrepreneur is full of challenges, victories, failures, and realizations. It is a path that requires perseverance, creativity, and an unyielding passion for one's vision. One of the notable figures in the entrepreneurial landscape who embodies these qualities is Max James. Known as the "King of Kiosks" and founder of American Kiosk Management Corporation, James' experiences are a valuable lesson for aspiring and seasoned entrepreneurs.

"The 7 Habits of Highly Successful Entrepreneurs" is more than just an article; it's a guidebook born out of Max James' real-life trials, triumphs, and tribulations. In his 60-year career, James has explored the dimensions of entrepreneurship, gaining insights that apply to anyone who wants to venture into the business world. Success begins with action. James emphasizes that you need an innate drive to achieve your goals. Determination to never give up is at the core of entrepreneurship, as evidenced by his perseverance in Vietnam. James's success in specialty retailing demonstrates the importance of trusting your own judgment. A life lesson from Vietnam: Resilience means moving forward with determination. Adaptability is critical. Failure is an opportunity for growth. Strategic growth is essential, with his kiosk business as a model.

Max James is not just an entrepreneur; he embodies the entrepreneurial spirit. His journey from a farm boy in Missouri to being shot down in Vietnam to building a billion-dollar company shows a life full of stories that inspire and teach. His book, *The Harder I Fall, The Higher I Bounce*, is a testament to his wisdom. But what makes James's story so compelling? His journey has never been easy. Whether he was fighting in Vietnam or struggling with his first startup, he faced adversity that would break many. His resilience and ability to learn from failure are not just buzzwords but lived experiences.

As the "King of the Kiosks," James revolutionized specialty retail. His intuitive understanding of customer needs and trust in his instincts paved the way for his international success. His willingness to share his insights with others reflects his commitment to nurturing the next generation of entrepreneurs. His article and book are profound teaching tools.

How can today's entrepreneurs benefit from James' lessons? His experiences underscore a mindset that goes beyond mere tactics. Being action-oriented, persistent, and resilient is both a strategy and a way of life. By embracing these traits, you can build a foundation for lasting success. His candid approach to his failures and his emphasis on

learning from them remind us that failure is not the end but a step toward growth. His insights into growth and the importance of knowing when to pivot or give up provide a nuanced understanding of business dynamics. His experiences with his kiosk business illustrate the delicate balance necessary to succeed in an ever-changing marketplace.

James continues to influence the world of entrepreneurs through his willingness to share, mentor, and lead. His story is a blend of business acumen and life wisdom. Whether on the battlefields of Vietnam or in the hectic world of retail, his journey is a role model for anyone looking to make a name for themselves in the business world.

Whether you're a seasoned entrepreneur or just starting your journey, Max James's lessons are a guide to success. His entrepreneurial spirit, perseverance, and wisdom are a timeless testament to what it takes to succeed on the challenging and rewarding path of entrepreneurship.

The article in question is more than a summary of his thoughts and experiences. It is a handbook, a collection of principles, ideas, and strategies proven to work in the real world. The principles are not abstract theories but lived experiences that have been shaped and refined through years of trial and error.

James' journey is filled with remarkable events and insights that make him stand out among his peers. His early life on the farm, the terrifying experience of being shot down in Vietnam and his subsequent rise in the business world are valuable lessons for anyone wanting to succeed. His experiences teach the importance of perseverance, resilience, and adaptability. He demonstrates the importance of learning from failure and how to turn setbacks into opportunities for growth.

In addition, his story shows the importance of staying true to your values and acting with integrity. His decisions, both in business and in life, reflect his commitment to honesty, hard work, and ethical behavior. He demonstrates that these values are moral virtues and essential components of successful business management.

James's story offers a broader perspective in a world where success often seems to be defined only by financial gain. He shows that success is about more than money; it's about creating value, building relationships, and positively impacting the world. He emphasizes the importance of mentorship, community, and social responsibility for anyone who wants to build a financially successful and socially responsible business.

In addition, his story illustrates the importance of vision and strategy in entrepreneurship. He demonstrates the importance of a clear vision combined with a well-defined strategy for long-term success. His ability to look beyond the immediate challenges and keep the big picture in mind helped him get through difficult times and ultimately achieve his goals.

As we dive deeper into James' story, we can find lessons that apply to business and life in general. His wisdom transcends the boundaries of entrepreneurship and offers relevant insights to anyone who wants to live a fulfilling and meaningful life.

Overall, the story of Max James is a powerful testament to the potential of the human spirit, determination, and ingenuity. His entrepreneurial journey, marked by ups and downs, successes, and failures, offers a wealth of knowledge and inspiration for anyone who wants to pursue their dreams and achieve their goals.

The lessons Max James learned in his life and career still resonate and inspire, and his legacy lives on as a beacon of hope and a source of wisdom for entrepreneurs and leaders from all walks of life. Whether you are just beginning your entrepreneurial journey or are already a seasoned leader, his insights and advice can provide valuable guidance and motivation as you navigate the challenges and opportunities of the entrepreneurial world.

For Don S. (No BHGEBH)

Jason Miller

JETLAUNCH
PUBLISHING

JETLAUNCH Publishing is for the growth-focused entrepreneur who wants to take their business to the next level by leveraging the power of a book. We take you from idea to a best-selling book to a fully automated business.

Find out how we can help you achieve that dream!

RAPIDLY GROW YOUR BUSINESS
with a bestselling book, course, and much more

Three Incredible Book Packages, Plus Exciting Extras

IGNITE **SIGNATURE** **APEX** **Add-Ons**

A better way to engage your customers

Your Customers Love Books

Unlike ads and email, they don't just throw them away. They're more likely to keep your book on their desk or bookshelf—right where they can see it every day.

Even if they never finish your book, you stay in their mind as someone who provides value and whom they can trust.

Engage your best customers with a book today!

What People Are Saying

"Chris and his team at JETLAUNCH did an amazing job with my latest book. I loved the professional design, and everyone on the team was friendly and helpful. I highly recommend using JETLAUNCH for all of your book needs. They are a joy to work with!"

– Dr. Joe Vitale

"Their customer support is lightning fast, the quality of their work is ON FIRE. If you want a book designed—use JETLAUNCH and IGNITE your project!"

John Lee Dumas

"JETLAUNCH is the real deal! They do not disappoint! Their design and communication skills are OVER THE TOP!"

Wendy Bryant

We are ready to help double your revenue.

Call Us: 520-561-0711

Email Us: chris@jetlaunch.net

jetlaunchpublishing.com

AN INTERVIEW WITH
MAX JAMES
BY CHRIS O'BYRNE

Chris:

Can you choose a story from your childhood that you think was instrumental in developing you into who you are today?

Max:

My dad was by far my greatest mentor. I grew up the son of a sharecropper and had to start by following two gray mules in the early days. Finally, we were able to get a tractor. Of course, only Dad drove the tractor. I was finally able to get rid of the two gray mules, and eventually, Dad let me drive the tractor.

I was out in the dusty field one day when the tractor stopped. I tried everything. I cleaned the carburetor and spark plugs; I did everything I thought you could do to get this thing started, but no luck. I look out across the field, and here comes a beat-up old pickup truck bouncing across this dusty field, and I thought, *This can't turn out very well for me.*

Dad got there and said, "Now, what the hell's wrong?" And I said, "Dad, I don't know. I've tried everything. I can't get it started."

He said, "Get out of the way." About five minutes later, the tractor's running fine. He turned to me and said, "I want you to remember this."

I said, "Yes, sir, what is it?"

He said, "Stay away from machinery. You don't know anything about wheelbarrows."

Not long after, Dad said, and I think this is important, "Look, you don't like this farm, do you?"

I said, "Yeah, I love the farm. I just don't like the farm work."

He said, "If you don't like something you're doing, you'll probably not be very good at it." I thought that was a great theory. He said, "I'm going to let you go."

I said, "Well, I don't know what that means."

And he said, "You're out of here. Go to town, and get yourself a job."

I did, and it was a great lesson. Dad fully supported my interests, whether they were extracurricular activities or schoolwork or a job. Overall, I learned a valuable lesson from him and explored a few of those in the book, which is why it's been essential for me to think back to what he said.

Dad was a recession-era baby from the old days, the depression era—and tight. Man,

he held onto every dime. People said he had the first dollar he ever made. One day, about the late 70s or early 80s, he told me, "Son, if there's something you want to do, you probably ought to go ahead and do it."

My mouth dropped open, and I said, "You mean spend money on something fun?"

He said, "Yeah. It's not because you won't be able to later; it's because you won't want to."

That was another valuable lesson. If something comes up that you think you want to do and it won't destroy your financial well-being, maybe you should go ahead and do it. I'm 81 years old now, and I have to tell you, he was right. Money's not a major problem anymore; however, the things that I can do, I find I just don't want to. I wish there were some things I had done earlier. That was a very valuable lesson in my early days.

Chris:

How long after that happened did you join the military?

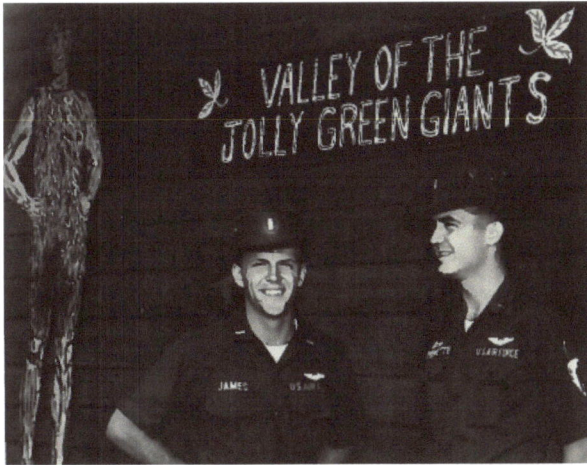

VALLEY OF THE JOLLY GREEN GIANTS

Max:

When I finally went to town and got a job, I was probably thirteen years old. I was blessed and got an appointment to the Air Force Academy when I was seventeen. Depending on your attitude, the timing was either good or not so good. I went to the academy, graduated, went to pilot training, and went to war, bing, bing, bing.

I volunteered to go over in rescue helicopters. My assignment was principally in Laos, but there was no war in Laos in 1966 and 1967. We hadn't told the world that we were there. I flew with the CIA and Air America, and we lived with Montagnard tribes most of the time, only seventy miles from Hanoi. We would go back to Thailand occasionally.

When the fighters, which we couldn't keep up with, left Thailand and headed into North Vietnam on their missions, we would join up with them at the Laotian-North Vietnam border. We'd follow them in, and if they got shut down, we would attempt to pick them up and bring them home.

The mission was the best in the world; it didn't matter what kind of war it was. "That Others May Live" was our mission. And we went in to bring these guys home so they could have a life, career, families, and children.

When they were shot down, they were three possibilities. The first was the possibility that they might not survive the explosion or crash. The second was capture and probably the Hanoi Hilton. And the third was me and the Jolly Green Rescue Organization. We were pretty popular, and we rescued about eighty percent of the people shot down in North Vietnam. At the time, our organization, the Air Rescue Organization, was the most decorated in the entire war. It was very rewarding. I had a fellow who sent me a case of scotch every Christmas for years for bringing him home.

I got shot down twice myself. People asked, "What is it like to get shot down?" It was the pits! I mean, it was terrible. What do you expect me to say? Oh, it was wonderful. I had a great time. No. It wasn't fun, but I made it home both times.

Chris:

Tell me about your transition to the business world.

Max:

The transition was not well planned. While I was still in Vietnam, the Air Force chose me to go back to graduate school in the field I wanted, which was management. When I got home, I flew to Randolph Air Force Base personnel training and was told I was going to Dayton, Ohio. I didn't want to go. I asked, "What's in Dayton, Ohio?" He said, "The Air Force School of Logistics Management." I replied, "Supply officer school? I'm a pilot. I don't want to become a supply officer." They said, "We've had these problems and don't think you can get in." I said, "I was on the dean's list every semester, but one. I think I can get in."

I went home, discouraged and depressed, and applied to all of the graduate schools for business and law and got accepted to all of them.

I returned to Randolph and said, "Hey, sergeant, I got good news and reviewed the bidding. And look, I got accepted." And he said, "Captain, I don't think you understand. You're going to Wright Patterson Air Force Base, the Air Force School of Logistics

Management, and you can't bluff the Air Force."

Ten days before registration at Stanford, I resigned from my commission, and I told this sergeant, "I'm going to Stanford either in a blue suit or blue jeans, and right now, I don't give a royal rat's ass which one it is." And so off I went—that was my transition.

I loved Stanford; I loved the biz school; I loved everything about it. I thought real estate was a wide-open field with a low-entry level I could enter. And that was my plan. I got a job and graduated, working for a fellow who many people claimed was the world's richest man at the time, and I managed all of his real estate worldwide. That was how I entered the real business world.

Chris:

Tell me about your current business. What is unique and valuable about it?

Max:

My current business is trying to help people who are failing in their businesses or want to move into their own businesses. After this mess with COVID, 30 percent of the people interviewed said they didn't want to go back to work but wanted to start their own business. There's a huge market out there for the entrepreneurial character.

I have said, "If you don't just absolutely, positively have to be an entrepreneur, don't do it." It's tough and the failure rate is high. Jack Canfield suggested I write a book about grit, determination, resilience, and bouncing back from failure by telling stories. So

my book is about all my failures along with humorous stories.

Two of the things I learned in business are crucial. If you're promoting or selling anything, your promotional material must be entertaining, or you'll lose people. Second, there must be a call to action for people to do something. If you have a great product and don't tell the world about it, it will probably not do well. And if you don't ask them to do something, such as buy your product or service, your business will fail. That's why I decided to tell humorous stories about my failures; I think they're funny, as most people do. There's a principle in each one of the stories about how I bounced back or what I should have done that I didn't, or I did do that I shouldn't have.

By the way, I call it an expensive hobby, trying to promote a book, but is not about marketing a book. However, the purpose of my business is to help people succeed by not making some of my mistakes.

I retired from my business in 2017, which was about six years ago. I sold that company to Nestle and had *"real money"*, which is fun. I told my wife, "We're going to retire now, live that dream about walking the beach hand in hand." And she said, "Well, I'm not retiring. *I'm too young to retire." I replied, "Whoa, whoa, whoa. Hang on a second. So what are we going to do?" And she said, "There is no we. I will start my own business now, and if I succeed, it'll be my success. And if I fail, it'll be my failure, and if I need your help, I'll ask you."* My wife who was *a major partner in the success of our company, American Kiosk Management (AKM) chose to start a new business in the specialty retail industry.* So she is a hair-on-fire entrepreneur now and has an international business going.

That's when Canfield asked me what I was going to do. And I said, "I don't know, but I hate retirement. It sucks." And he said, "Why don't you write a book about all your failures? You're a great storyteller. See if you can put it from verbal onto paper." I didn't know if I could do that, but I guess it turned out okay. We've won many awards and made the Amazon bestseller list in four countries. So that's kind of my business now, trying to learn how to get these principles out to people, which I believe will help many people, particularly the entrepreneurial.

Jack Canfield told me, "Max, don't limit your market to just entrepreneurs." There are too many great life lessons in there that can apply to more than entrepreneurs, particularly small businesses and families." Fortunately, I don't need the money, so I'm trying to get the word out about these principles that I hope will be very helpful to people.

The title of my book is *The Harder I Fall, The Higher I Bounce.*

Some friends who were kind enough to write endorsements said it all. "Max, you have bounced from one impossible situation to the next improbable situation. And somehow or another, you always just keep climbing the mountain."

In the last company, we made $1.8 billion in sales over a reasonably short period. From following those gray mules, old Tom and old Jack, to selling a company that did that well in the market, I guess it is a story of many failures and a few good successes.

Chris:

Who were some of the key influences or mentors in your life?

Max:

Well, my dad is number one. My dad had a twin brother. In fact, he had five brothers. One was a twin, and that brother went off to college. They lived on the adjacent farm with their dad. And my dad, I think, looking back now, was undereducated but wise. I think he must have had ADD, quite honestly. He didn't do well in school. His dad told him when he was in the ninth or tenth grade, "Look, obviously, this book learning isn't working for you, so just quit school and come back and work on the farm." So my dad had a tenth-grade education, sort of, but was wise, and I'm trying to point out his wisdom in the book. He was my first great mentor.

Dad entered the cavalry in World War II because he knew about horses and mules.

But he also had an additional duty; he trained the officer's polo ponies. Can you believe the officers in the Army used to have polo ponies? Well, my dad didn't know anything about polo, but he could teach the horses tricks to rear up and lay down, and the guys would get behind the horse like they were shooting bad guys.

We always had horses. I started when I was three years old and had a pony. Once, my dad bought a new horse, and I was going to take it on a Saturday and ride up to my cousin's house, which was a few miles away. As I left, Dad was in the front yard, and he asked where I was going. I said, "I'm just going to trade some comic books with my cousins."

Off I went down this gravel road. I had to cross a rickety old bridge to get to my cousin's house, and when I got up there, the horse wouldn't cross. I kicked him, ran at it, and the horse reared every time. Finally, I got off and tried to lead the horse across. It wouldn't lead.

So I said to myself, *I guess I'm not going up to my cousin's place on this new horse.* I returned home and thought, *Oh God, I hope Dad's not there because he will say I let the horse beat me, so what kind of horseman am I?* But sure enough, I get in the front yard back home, and there he is. He looks up at me and says, "What happened? I thought you were going up to your cousin's."

I thought, *I can lie, or I can tell the truth. Both are bad options.* I chose to lie. So I said, "Oh, I don't know, Dad. I don't think they've been to the grocery store and gotten any new comics. And so I just decided..." He said, "The horse wouldn't cross the bridge, would it?" He saw right through me. I said, "Dad, listen, I tried everything. I couldn't get the horse to cross."

So he reaches up, grabs me by the waist, swings up behind me on the saddle, kicks the horse in the withers with his plow shoes, and off we go. We get to the bridge, and the horse refuses to cross. Dad tries two or three times, but the horse won't cross.

He said, "Get off the horse." I was happy to get off. He tried it again. The horse wouldn't cross the bridge. So Dad says, "You see that tree branch over there? Hand it to me." I don't know if he was going to use it on me or the horse, but I handed him the branch. He headed across the bridge, and hit the horse right between his ears. The horse stumbled around a bit; Dad ran him up to the bridge, and the horse stumbled across. Dad turned the horse around and came right back across, got off the horse, and told me to get on. He handed me the branch, and I thought, *Horse, please cross this bridge because I don't want to do what Dad just did.*

I got up to the bridge and waved the stick so the horse could see it. The horse's ears were straight back and it was looking more at me than the bridge—or trying to. Then we crossed the bridge. *Oh, thank God. Come on, horse, go. We got to go one more tiime.* I went back and crossed the bridge again. Dad didn't say anything; he just swung behind me in the saddle and said, "Let's go home."

Once we got home, he swung off, looked up at me, and said, "I expect you'll be going to your cousin's house now, aren't you?" I said, "Yes, sir."

When I got to my cousin's house, he asked, "Where have you been? I've been waiting on you forever." I said, "My dad was teaching me something about horsemanship."

Here's the real point. When you meet a serious obstacle in life, there are two things to remember. Number one, you may need some help, and you better find it. Number two, you may have to use a little pressure. Hopefully, you won't have to hit anybody in the head with a branch, but you may need to be resilient, have grit, and force your way. It may not take physical punishment, but it may take some real courage to defeat those you're negotiating with or at least find a solution.

I could name twenty or more other mentors, including people at the Air Force Academy. I was lucky enough to be an administrative assistant to my congressman while I was supposed to be in high school, and I wasn't. So I went to Washington as a seventeen-year-old.

I had a great mentor officer at the Air Force Academy who taught me great things about delegating authority but not delegating responsibility. If something goes wrong in your organization, be it military, business, or whatever, that you didn't even know was happening or had happened, it's still your responsibility, and you've got to fix it or settle it somehow or another.

I've used that principle in all my organizations since the Air Force Academy, and I've preached it to the people who have worked for and with me to let them know that there weren't any excuses. Hopefully, there would be reasons, but it was still their responsibility.

I worked for an attorney who taught me a lot about dealing with the legal profession.

He was a great mentor. And then my failures were my best mentors. Also, a lawyer who got me through many of those failures was a great mentor. And by the way, he is still my attorney after thirty years.

Chris:

What would you say has been one of the most valuable lessons you have learned?

Max:

Responsibility is probably number one on my list. You will need help; you can't get through life or business without it. First, find people you can trust, who are hopefully willing to help you, either for free or for a fee. Second, hire for character and train for skill. If you hire people who turn out to have poor character, you will have nothing but trouble.

So hire for character. Find hard-charging people with high integrity, good solid character, and morals and train them. When you make a mistake, cut your losses early. Don't just try to fix people because you believe you can. You don't have time for that. Do what you can. Be generous, but cut your losses early. If you find somebody of poor character, it's not your job to change their character, not as an employer or a business owner. That isn't going to work. Hire for character, train for skill, and cut your losses early. These are the important lessons in business.

Chris:

How do you know when you have found somebody of good character?

Max:

Well, the easy answer is they don't do anything dumb, stupid, illegal, or questionable from a morality point of view. So number one is a negative approach in that you look for what is not present. Okay, this guy's doing great, and nothing's going wrong.

The way you find out otherwise is you have controlling data. It's called walking the manufacturing floor. You can't just sit up in the warehouse in your little office and watch the manufacturing floor. You need to get out there. You need to know your people. Learn about them and how they are doing. Data collection on a very direct basis is important.

What set apart my last company that did so well apart, the $1.8 billion company, was

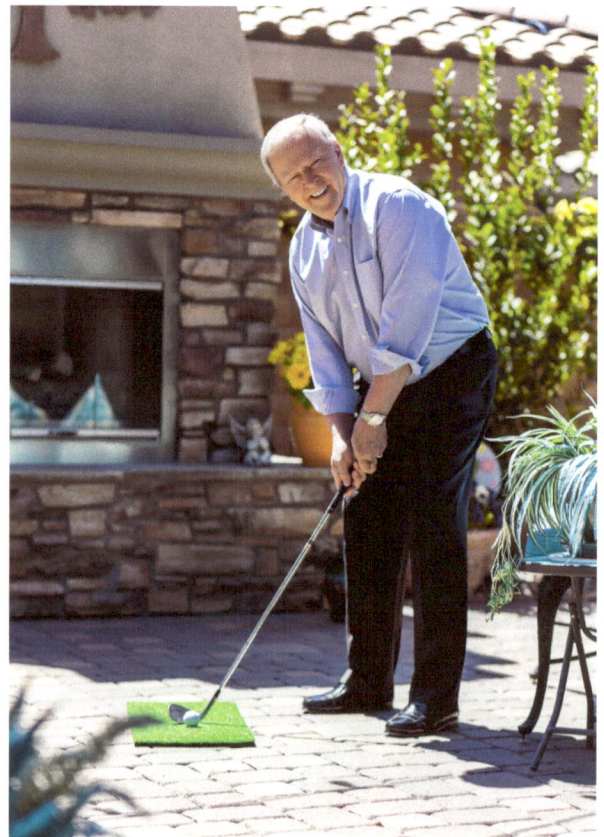

that we had 400 manned locations and shopping centers worldwide and 800 of what they call "automated retail." I used to call them vending machines, but now, it's called automated retail. So how do you control it? How do you monitor? How do you train when training is needed? You see those kiosks and carts in locations with only three or maybe four employees, and normally only one at a time at a kiosk in the mall down the hallways.

to help them avoid temptation? That's what we believed in. Or do you create situations where they are tempted and steal from you? That's why we had many locations doing so well with a great product.

We chose to try to remove the temptation. I don't want people to get in trouble. The reports would come in, and if the bank deposit didn't match, we would call the

We developed reporting systems and monitoring systems so we would know if the bank deposit you made each night didn't match the net sales. We would know if you didn't sign out for your break, which was legally required. We would know through our reporting. Do you want to create systems

next morning and say, "Here's a chance to explain. What happened?" Maybe somebody borrowed $5 because they needed gas money to get home. Then two weeks later, the baby needs medicine, and they borrow $100, fully intending to give it back. But since nobody caught it, next time, they think, *I might be able to get that new, used car, and no one will know.* And we had examples of where people took us for a lot of money, but we caught it and prosecuted.

We felt like that was good for them, and it certainly was good for the rest of the company. Macy's is the one that taught me that. You don't do wrong at Macy's without being prosecuted. And so I think that set us apart. That led us to become the world's largest specialty retailer. And so we felt like that was the secret sauce to our ability to open so many geographical locations and still control the company. Remove the temptation. That was my system for controlling remote locations.

Chris:

What parting wisdom do you have for people?

Max:

Number one, read my book. The whole purpose of the stories is to help people. I tried to put what I felt was wisdom from experience and failures into the book. If you want to do something, whether it's business or philanthropy, of which I'm a great fan—just do it.

There's a bestselling book of all times translated into more languages than any book ever that says, "If you give, it will return 10-fold." In another place, it says, "If you give, it'll return 100-fold." I think that's true, and I practice that. We did it as a company and I've done it as an individual. One of the great rewards of success is giving back.

Maybe it's money; maybe it's time; maybe it's your experience; whatever it is, practice that. You won't always be able to spend money. Still, we've probably given away 80 percent of everything I've made to a camp for terminally ill kids, and a building at the Air Force Academy, The Center for Character and Leadership Development. It's not all about yourself. It's about sharing your blessings with those who haven't been so blessed or so lucky.

In another word of advice, you weren't put here because it would be easy. Grab your britches, pull them up, and pour into this thing. Yes, you will fail; that's part of the deal. Some of us think we were put here to learn, so you must have grit. There's a great book by Angela Duckworth called *Grit*. Sometimes, just grin and bear it and push on. When you fall, that's painful, but climbing that mountain is so much fun. So just get up, dust yourself off, and start back up. Create a new path up the mountains, making it easier for folks behind you to go up that same path to whatever their version of success is. Enjoy life, but tackle it with determination because it ain't always easy.

Action Steps

1. Follow the author's advice on hiring practices and focus on character, not just skills. Your organization can benefit from this approach by seeking employees with high integrity, good morals, and strong character, and then training them for the specific skills needed. This can lead to a more trustworthy and cohesive team and reduce the potential for internal problems.

2. Implement systematic monitoring and reporting in your organization as described by the author. By developing systems to track and reconcile your operations, such as sales and bank deposits, you can ensure better control and accountability. Resisting the temptation to closely monitor transactions can lead to fewer mistakes and unfair practices in your business.

3. Look at failure and resilience as learning opportunities, as the author has pointed out. Recognize that failure is an essential part of growth and success in business. Your determination, perseverance and willingness to tackle challenges head-on can turn obstacles into learning experiences. Foster a culture that celebrates perseverance and innovation, and keep working toward your goals even when you face setbacks.

About the Author

Max James is an American author and serial entrepreneur, best known as the founder of The American Kiosk Management company and dubbed "The King of Kiosks" by Fortune magazine. He is the author of the award-winning book *The Harder I Fall, The Higher I Bounce*, a business memoir for today's entrepreneur and business executives. Max shares his journey from growing up on a farm, to being shot down in Vietnam, to creating a billion-dollar company.

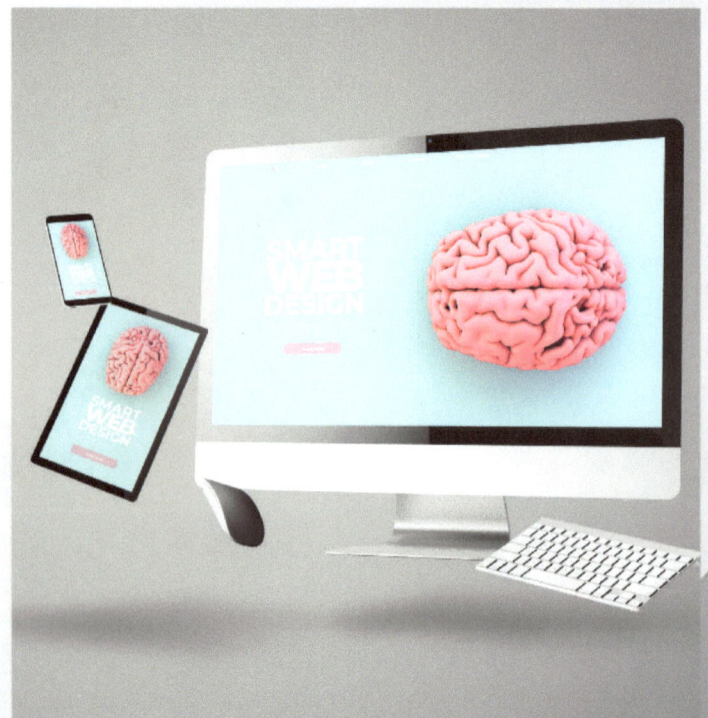

THE 7 HABITS OF
HIGHLY SUCCESSFUL
ENTREPRENEURS

MAX JAMES

Max James shares 60 years of business success, failures, and the inevitable truths all entrepreneurs must learn along the way.

Something shifted in me while attending Stanford University back in the early 70s. As I was working towards my MBA, instead of writing about successful businesses, I gravitated towards companies that had failed, yet somehow found success. The ability to overcome failure after failure intrigued me.

Over a 60 year career, I can honestly say, it feels like I've tried every single one of those tactics that I studied.

Here are the lessons I've learned through 6 decades as a businessman and entrepreneur, and the mindset all start-up owners must have.

1. Action-Driven

What separates entrepreneurs from regular people? Building a business from scratch, when no one else can see or agree with your vision, requires an innate drive from within that says, "I MUST do this. I have no choice! There are no other acceptable options!"

The simple answer is that every business story starts with the founder seeing something missing in the marketplace or something that he or she knows they can improve upon and thus choses to attempt to provides it. From Henry Ford to Elon Musk. From William Randolph

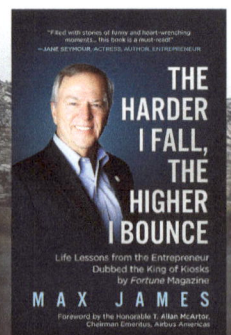

Hearst to Arianna Huffington. Great ideas are just that, a great idea...until an entrepreneur takes action to development it, create a company around it, and turn it into a successful venture. From Angela Duckworth's book, "Grit", we learn:

"Talent x Effort = Skill,
Skill x Effort =Achievement"!

2. Tenacity

The Oxford Dictionary definition of the word tenacity is "the quality or fact of being very determined." It also means persistence. In other words, entrepreneurs never give up. They accept failure, learn from it and quickly bounce back and move on.

I was shot down twice in Vietnam. The second time was scarier because we didn't know if the village we crashed landed in was friend or enemy. At one point, all I could do was put my fears aside and rely on my training. I was never going to give up in getting me and my colleagues back to base.

That training, especially at the US Air Force Academy, gifted me with a significant ability to handle extreme stress. And that is the secret tonic. Life is stressful enough, but being an entrepreneur requires the effort to accept another level of challenges.

If you want to be an entrepreneur, you must learn to accept and manage stress. You have to be mentally and emotionally prepared to make the decisions that are required to move as quickly as possible in going from startup to a stable business.

3. Trust Your Instincts

Fortune Magazine called me the King of Kiosks, due to our company becoming the largest international retailer in the Specialty Retail industry. Once we began selling a new product line that was marketed via infomercials on television, it became critical that we establish training programs, customer loyalty incentives and kiosk vending machines. Linda Johansen-James, my partner, built a phenomenal team that under her leadership achieved tremendous success.

Although the trend was technology driven, as people moved to Amazon and other online websites, we noticed that our customers were different. They liked the one-on-one face time with us. Since we were selling Proactiv, many of our customers became life-long advocates simply because they wanted a compassionate face with whom to talk. And the results Proactiv gave them inspired them to tell others.

When new technology arises, you have to embrace it wholeheartedly, including taking a step back for a moment and looking closely at what your customers want, as well as anticipating those things that would not be effective for them.

That means you have to trust in your own decision making capabilities. Look, we all have doubts from time-to-time. But make a decision, stick to it, and only change when new information shows up.

If we had abandoned our carts in favor of technology only sales, we wouldn't have sold billions of dollars all over the world.

Trust yourself. You got this.

4. Resilience

There is an old saying, "If you are walking through hell, keep on going." I learned this firsthand in Vietnam. But that was war. Moving forward with grit and determination and perseverance should become your new mantra.

We now live in a day and age where people are upset by words. Words!? Whose words are you hearing? DOUBT YOUR DOUBTS, DO NOT DOUBT YOUR DREAMS! Do you honestly believe you have what it takes to bounce back from failure? Are you going to give up at the first sign of failure? Remember that "FAILURE IS NEVER FINAL!"

True grit is about perseverance and unwavering effort. It's about developing the skills you need and staying focused on the long-term goals you've set. After being knocked down are you capable of sticking with your vision of success no matter what?

Again always remember, failure is never final, and SUCCESS IS NEVER ENDING! Stay focused on your vision.

5. Know When To Pivot

Pivot is the hot buzz word nowadays, but it's much, much more than that. It's about having the guts to pause, reassess, listen to feedback from the market, then look for what is profitable and what is not...and if appropriate, "pivot" and if necessary, change directions.

Not always easy I can tell you. When John Chambers, former CEO of Cisco realized back in the early 2000s that the company was in trouble, Cisco's stock went from $89 a share and plunged to $11, he took action.

On self-reflection and assessment, John realized that he was the bottleneck at Cisco. Every decision was made through him. It would take weeks for things to get his approval. He realized he was the problem and he removed himself from the day-to-day decision making.

Speed was necessary in this moment in order to save Cisco. John eliminated over 3,000 products that no longer served the Cisco brand and shifted autonomy of the organization to two groups—whose main job was to scout for companies and hardware they could add to their bottom line.

That pivot grew Cisco from $1.9 billion to $49.2 billion in yearly revenue.

Look, you may not be in the big leagues yet like Cisco, but when you are building from the ground up, every decision will

be reflected from your own personal talent, experience, and effort.

As a start up, you will soon discover that if you have problems in your personal life, it may also affect your professional life, and vice versa. That's why great entrepreneurs and you should never stop working on your personal development, learning from your mistakes and pivoting according to the marketplace demands.

6. Know When To Quit, but Don't Burn Your Bridges.

My first startup was Executorial Services. It was similar to WeWorks except that I started in the 70s while at Stanford. And It failed miserably!

The owner of the building that I was leasing space from went bankrupt. So as he stopped providing services to me, I had to be honest with my subtenants; I couldn't guarantee basic services like toilet paper and electricity.

It was outside influences that I didn't have control over that caused the business to fail. I didn't get angry or try to get even. I was already in hot water as I took on the risk. But after talking with my lawyer, I realized I could settle with a buyout.

If I had lost my temper, I would have never been able to find a solution to the problem of getting out of the lease. And I would have never found a life-long friend in my lawyer.

I recommend Seth Godin's book "The Dip: The Extraordinary Benefits of Knowing When to Quit (and When to Stick)". It's packed with case studies of companies that stopped selling for a few months, reassessed, then refocused. Again, "Failure Is Never Final".

7. Learn From Failure

You may not want to hear this, but I've learned more from my failures than my successes. But failure is meaningless unless you sit back and do a deep dive into "why?" you failed.

You can delegate authority, but you cannot delegate responsibility. If I am the cause of a failed business, then I need to face that fact, and change. If others in my venture are the cause, then I need to accept the responsibility and focus on my personal accountability. That may require learning a new skill or choosing a consultant or business partner that has the skillset that you lack.

Multiple streams of income starts with your ability to handle more, delicate more, and learn from your hiccups on the road to success.

8. BONUS: Focus on Growth

We used to have a saying at my company; "Go like Hell. Pause. Then clean up the mess."

When Linda Johansen started working at AKM, she made sure that she or a qualified trainer/manager was onsite and present for every single cart we set up across the country and internationally. We grew like gangbusters because Linda and her team had the ability to deliver to our customer what they really wanted.

But the real growth came even with a tight schedule. We trained people quickly and thoroughly. Our philosophy was "hire for character and train for skill and cut your losses early". Then we moved onto open the next kiosk or cart in the next state or next shopping mall. At one point we opened a new location every other day.

But we didn't abandon the original managers and salespeople. Daily meetings revised and repetitive training until we knew our staff was confident.

And the proof was in our employee loyalty. Many of our managers were still with us after 17 years. A milestone in the retail world.

I hope this list helps. Make sure you reach out to me with any questions. I look forward to your success.

NONPROFIT OF THE MONTH: VETCARES

What a vet doesn't know about home ownership...

What would later become VetCares was born of sister company, USA Homeownership Foundation, Inc (DBA VAREP or Veterans' Association of Real Estate Professionals—you know the military loves their acronyms).

They were a nonprofit focused on educating real estate professionals on VA loans and successful homeownership so vets could get homes and live the American dream. It was a highly needed entity as they had found that vets were being turned away in droves (some almost flatly discriminated against) if they tried to use the VA benefit.

The founder simply wanted more education so more vets could get into homes and use the benefits they earned on and off the battlefield. This would grow into numerous chapters about the nation, with 80% of members being military.

Not content with that, they started multiple programs, including the **Stop, Drop, and Push** campaign to end veteran suicide. That was received so passionately by all members that he wanted to start a purely philanthropic event in education and healing that was not limited to real estate. He said it was the members, though, who brought the passion.

One of those is Carla Lemon. As a top realtor specializing in VA loans, she was invited to join the meeting on the first chapter for VAREP. She volunteered for five years and then was offered a job with the National Corporate Office as the Assoc Director (a blessing that would mean a considerable pay drop), which she took. Continually succeeding in the mission, she was offered a couple of years later the executive directorship, and then finally, she was asked to launch VetCares and be its executive director.

So, I had to ask Carla what makes her do what she does.

"We help closing costs for low to moderate buyers. That alone is enough," she said. But then stopping slightly as it obviously had moved her emotionally, she added, "We gave a $2,000 gift to someone in dire need. They got the home, got the keys, and moved in. Without that blessing, they would not have been able to close the house. We have stepped in because of a lost job, and they feared eviction or utilities being cut. That's when VetCares can move on it."

If you have a business, you can support VetCares in pretax dollars. Click the link below or use the QR code, and we'll show you how to fund support from these brave men and women rather than funding the system.

For more information:

Carla Lemon
951-444-7361
clemon@vetcares.org
vetcares.org

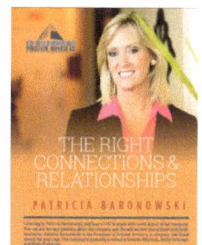

START YOUR OWN COMMUNITIES

MIKE STEWARD

My company is called Vision Fox Business Advisors and is designed to help small and midsize business owners meet their goals. The business has three main divisions.

The first division is the business brokerage where we help mid-size businesses go to market, put their marketing package together, find what a buyer profile looks like, and then begin marketing their business confidentially. We work with prospects who come in looking to buy a business similar to what we've described in a generic sense. We qualify the prospects and get them to sign nondisclosure agreements, working them through the process that we have to help them make a decision, go through due diligence, and eventually purchase the business that we have listed and transfer ownership.

The second division is business coaching. Through coaching, we help some of those same potential buyers, or in some cases sellers, understand how to grow their businesses and make their businesses more valuable. We also help them get away from the daily grind of being in the business like they had to be when they first started as founders. We help them graduate into more of a C-level type of position within their business.

And then the third division is helping franchise owners grow their franchises, sell their franchises, or compare franchises, looking at where their personality and skill sets may fit to plug into a franchise system as a means of being an entrepreneur. That's really kind of what it boils down to.

What sets me apart is my experience and perspective. I have started a few businesses from scratch on my own. I have also helped transition businesses from private or independent brands into franchise brands. I work with about thirty franchise owners as their business coach, and I think what sets me apart is my breadth of experience of being in their shoes but not being too close to the business.

I owned a business for several years with my ex-wife. As business partners, we lost focus on other things in our lives and got buried in the business. So, I've been in those shoes, and now I know how to get out of that situation and help others do the same.

I really help owners have a different perspective. That is probably what I'm best at—offering that different perspective to help them get their business sold or help them grow their business.

The role of community in business is twofold. One, helping business owners understand where they fit in the community. And by that, I mean that I've worked with several

prospective buyers for businesses that had been listed, and the business just wasn't the right fit for them. From a community standpoint, I don't think that they could award (you may want to remove award and put "have worn" that badge of being the owner of that business within their community because it wasn't in line with who they were, or who they even wanted to evolve into.

The second role of community is the role it plays for me. I've always been involved in my local community. I'm the president of several boards and volunteer within business-specific industries that I've been in. Being involved in my community has helped me personally develop, and I have always received double whatever I give when I get involved in a community.

Recently, as we've all evolved into the digital world even more due to COVID, I am now finding the groups of people that I want to be involved with digitally, which I find just awesome. I have friends in Australia who I never would have met. We exchange ideas. We exchange personal stuff, and we now have access to a bigger community that we probably didn't have access to before COVID.

When it comes to specific digital communities, I am involved in LinkedIn and Facebook. Facebook is a completely different community where I engage with business owners on a more personal level. When I became a certified life coach (I'm also a certified business coach), my coach at the time chuckled and said that life and business are the same from a coaching standpoint because they all mesh together. Your personal problems come to work, and your work problems come to life.

I find that LinkedIn is quite a bit different than Facebook for building a community. Although we may talk a little bit differently on LinkedIn and showcase in different ways, those same people often share different aspects of their life on Facebook in a different manner. Those are my two biggest online communities. Locally, I'm involved with the Chamber of Commerce on kind of a big level and see how different businesses are performing based on our local economy.

Another thing that I don't always think about as a community, but it absolutely is, is my podcast. The main reason I started my podcast is that I get to speak to some really cool people.

For instance, if I list a business for sale, and let's say fifty prospects come looking at the business, there are some really cool people in that mix of fifty. Some disappear, and we don't engage at a deep level, but they are all fascinating: the experiences they've had, where they've lived, the goals that they haven't met, the goals that they *have* met, and where they came from.

And the same with business sellers. I get an intimate look at why they're selling their business, how they started their business, and behind-closed-doors types of insight into their life. Often that's transitioning into retirement or relocating or some other neat event that we all dream of hitting those milestones in different ways.

Additionally, the people who seek coaching are incredibly interesting people, and so is

where they're trying to take their lives to. I found that I have a tremendous amount of intrigue and respect for the variety of businesspeople in my life. I wanted to be able to share those experiences, and that was the whole reason behind the podcast.

I essentially created the foundation out of a few canned questions, like how do you stay healthy? And I think secretly, when we see somebody who's grinding out a tough lifestyle of entrepreneurship, we all want to know what they're doing that we're not that maybe we can learn and grow from. Or what KPIs do they have in their business? And how did they go from zero to X in five years?

The premise is to engage and have a great conversation. I've had great conversations with people over the years by engaging with a variety of businesspeople, but to strategically have that with some very interesting folks creates three opportunities.

One opportunity is to motivate. Maybe there's an entrepreneur out there who just needs to hear that they're not alone. The second is to share ideas. There have been some incredible health and wellness ideas that have come out of my podcast. The third is letting other entrepreneurs and business owners see through the lens of another business owner and view how they're positioning their lifestyle for success.

My first word of advice for starting an online community would be to truly understand your purpose for starting an online community. You must know what you are trying to accomplish. I think getting clear on that is the first step because that drives all your other actions.

The second would be to move forward. That's often my advice with coaching clients or business sellers: If you understand the purpose, move forward today, and not a month from now. Today is the day to move forward, but only if you know the purpose of it.

Third would be to go wide. There are a lot of really cool people out there you can find if you're open minded. I'll go back to the example of my friend in Australia. He and I could easily have never met, but we did, and he introduced me to another person in Texas, and without him, she and I never would have met. So, go wide enough within whatever connects back to your purpose to make sure you're not excluding those who could add value.

The last thing that comes to mind is to be open to variety in your community. Maybe that's similar to going wide, but I've learned so much from people in different industries that I know makes me better both in business and personally. Be open minded and pay attention to make sure it aligns with your purpose, but it doesn't have to be super niched to have a community that aligns with whatever your focus is.

To get involved in a local community, I suggest you find something meaningful to you, and that could mean so many different things. Meaningful could mean rescuing animals. It could be a health concern or health related, or it could be something that directly relates to your business.

I've always been very involved in the national, state, and local associations of realtors. When I had a real estate company, I felt like that industry gave so much to my family and me that I wanted to give back.

I've always tried to live in such a way that whatever I take from, I give at least an equal

amount back. My driver at that point was to make sure that I was contributing to something that contributes to me. That kept me driven to keep engaging.

I get way more out of being involved in that community in probably fifteen different aspects of my life than just that specific industry. Therefore, I think the most important thing you can do is find something meaningful to you for whatever reason it may be. It may be going in with non-selfish motives, but I can guarantee you will leave with more than you brought unintentionally.

It's important to understand, before you even get out of bed, what the purpose of your day is. That's kind of a big statement, but you must know at least your broad purpose for the day. What's your reason to wake up in the morning and put your feet on the ground? Almost everyone has to-do list of some sort, but make sure your day is meaningful.

I have an alarm that goes off on my phone every morning at 8:30, and it's a reminder to create meaning and value. It says, "Be Intentional. Live, Love, and Matter." I try to live every day with that mantra. That would probably be my best advice, whether it pertains to running a business or being part of a community or just engaging with your family.

My "why" is *freedom*. For me, that covers so many things. That means freedom from having to depend on healthcare when I'm seventy years old. That's the hope to have rules in my life that help me operate in a fashion that allows me not to be dependent on healthcare, whether it's medical needs or prescriptions. That means freedom from being able to make the right decisions of what type of work I want to do and to make sure that I'm able to do meaningful, enjoyable, fun work most of the time on my terms. I want the freedom to do that versus having to just get a job or take a job or take a new client.

It also means the freedom to make choices that align with what I expect out of each day and what I expect of my remaining years left on earth to play this wonderful game we get to play every day.

I have a fifteen-year-old son, and I'm showing him examples that supersede the examples I was shown and that's not always easy. I'm trying to upgrade his life to make sure he sees the best way, at least the best way I have the means to understand, of what life should look like.

Mike Steward has been coaching business professionals in various roles since 2001. In addition to his own startups and acquisitions, he has helped many owners and sales professionals across industries grow their businesses. He has started and operated five new businesses from inception to exit. In addition, he has helped launch two major franchise brands while staying on as a COO, President, and Vice President during post-launch stages. During the past fourteen years, he has worked closely with close to one hundred business owners in the ever-changing industry of real estate.

mikesteward.com

STRATEGIC GROWTH PROFESSIONALS

We Help Your Business Grow

CONSULTING AGENCY

SERVICE

Online courses

Our courses are strategically designed to assist your business in being recognized by customers, thereby growing your business and achieving long-term revenue streams, as well as how to maintain your competitive edge

Certifications and Contracts

SGP helps you in successfully navigating the complicated path of government contracting by assisting you in obtaining any government certifications you may qualify for and throughout the proposal lifecycle.

Holistic Grant Proposals

Our comprehensive grant proposal services focus on the entire lifecycle, including the development of a repository system.

ABOUT US

At Strategic Growth Professional you are not considered clients, you are considered partners. When we begin working together, it is our partnership that makes each of us successful.

WHY CHOOSE US ?

We are a team of experts and have helped hundreds of people grow their businesses. We have assisted our partners in obtaining over $2 billion in federal, state, and local government contract awards, $1 billion in federal, state, local, foundation, and corporate grant awards, and another $1 billion in private sector awards.

Partnering with you in success

Emily J. McIntyre
Strategic Growth Professionals
O: 719.504.4190
C: 719.257.1981
info@strategicgrowthprofessionals.com
www.strategicgrowthprofessionals.com

HELPING OTHERS THROUGH COMMUNITY

MIKE JACKSON

Jason Miller (the founder of Strategic Advisor Board) and I were infantrymen together a million years ago. It's been a while, but I remember. I had a midlife crisis, and I decided being an infantryman wasn't hard enough. So, I thought I should be a US Army Special Forces medic who also spoke Arabic.

I spent two years in training to become that. The course alone was fifty weeks long. It covered everything from clinical medicine to doing surgery and anesthesia, and I've used a lot of that overseas during my work. After getting qualified to do the work, I did that for twenty-seven years.

That opened a lot of doors and opportunities. My last active-duty job was teaching the two-week medical refresher that all Special Operations medics and all the services have to attend every two years. I taught that for about six years.

Halfway through that six-year period, I retired and became a contractor. I did a couple of different jobs at the Special Operations Medical School as a contractor. I did the regular medical refresher, and I helped build a surgical med refresher course.

Now I teach surgery and anesthesia full-time. Working in that Special Operations arena, I've had tons of wonderful opportunities to work with other service people. I work with a couple of Air Force retired aerospace medical doctors, and I teach jungle and dive medicine, usually in St. Croix, US Virgin Islands.

I also work with a local Boy Scout troop as their wilderness survival merit badge guy. Whenever they need a wilderness survival merit badge course run, I run that.

I am also an American Red Cross certified instructor, so I teach a wilderness and remote first aid course for Boy Scouts and Boy Scout leaders in the area. It's a fun sixteen-hour course and includes a lot about working in the woods. I get to use my experience from being a medic overseas to help guide my teaching, and it's a lot of fun.

I teach both in person and online. I help out with the Special Forces Medical Sergeant course on Fort Bragg at the Joint Special Operations Medical Training Center.

People ask me, "Have you ever had to do this overseas?" When they ask this, however, we're usually in a solid operating room with full sterile protocols. So I say, "The last time I did this overseas, I had a ballcap on, I was under a tarp outside, and had a cigar in my mouth. I had sterile gloves on, and that was about as sterile as I could be with the equipment I had. Sometimes you just got to pump them full of more antibiotics because you have nothing else to do for them."

I primarily worked in Iraq and spent multiple years there. There are five Special Forces groups, and each group has an area of responsibility in the world. Some work in Southeast Asia, some work in Europe, some work in Africa, some work in central South America—all over the world. The group I picked was the one that spoke Arabic in southwest Asia, so that's where I spent a lot of time.

I have been very lucky, because I've never had to do major work on any of my guys.

That's where I come from. I also run a Special Forces mentoring group for the young, up-and-coming Special Forces medics in the course. My goal is to help them be less jacked-up than I was when I first got to a team. Another guy and I have been doing that since 2018. I think between the two of us, we've only missed maybe three times in four or five years; I really take that community and commitment very seriously.

And it's crazy, but I'll get a phone call from, say, Romania, and it's some Special Forces medic who has a question. Honestly, I'm the last person anybody needs a call to ask medical advice, but it really does make me feel good when somebody calls me and asks for it.

I can usually answer their questions, but if not, I can at least send them away to somebody who can, but I do take it very seriously. In 2013, I started working on a presentation I would give at the end of the two-week med refresher course I teach. Over the years, it's increased from thirty minutes to two hours. And for every two-week med refresher course, I'm the last guy that they hear. I get guys all the time calling me, texting me, or emailing me and saying, "Hey, I messed up," or "Hey, a guy on my team's messed up. How can you help me fix them?"

I retired from the US Army seven years ago, but they still let me be a part of that community. I have a Signal chat room that's maxed out at 1,000 Special Forces medics. People ask me questions, but I also ask questions. One time, I responded, "Hey, this is the answer. I'm Mike Jackson, nice to work with you." And one of the best compliments I ever heard was his response. He said, "Everybody

I've never had any of my guys shot and had to fix him. I've been very, very lucky. Unfortunately, I've had to work on other fellow American service members.

I think every time I ever worked on an American service member, it was a roughest time because it was important. It didn't matter what was going on around me, if bullets were flying around over my head because I could turn all that stuff off. And all I did was focus on the patient. Those were rough times.

I relate more with the Special Forces medical community than the Special Forces community because that's the community in which I served and in which I now teach.

knows who you are, Mike. You're the OG of Special Forces medicine." And I was like, "Wow, I don't know if I'm actually the OG; there are plenty other people who have been at it longer than me." But that felt good.

That ages me a lot, and I know that sooner or later I have to grow up. I will probably have to leave here and do something better for me. When I have to cross that line, it's going to be a rough. I can't do this forever; I know that.

I am also involved in some local communities. I work with a Boy Scout group out of Columbia, SC, which is about two and a half hours away. I met a guy who was a physical therapist at a wilderness medicine course, and his son was an Eagle Scout in that group.

All the Boy Scout leaders need to be wilderness and remote-first aid-certified through the American Red Cross. Boy Scouts can also attend that course. I run those courses about three times a year as needed for everybody on the south end of North Carolina and the north end of South Carolina in about a two-and-a-half-hour bubble. There is a small Boy Scout camp called Camp Coker in South Carolina, and we usually run it out there. It's a beautiful spot with a big lake and lots of land.

I used to volunteer for the American Red Cross teaching classes for them, but they're a really weird organization. They would rather pay an instructor to teach classes for them than to have somebody volunteer to teach those classes for free. They stopped having any kind of volunteer teach any classes out of my hometown for the American Red Cross, and all they do is pay

instructors to teach classes. I don't do this because I want the money; I do because I want to help people save people's lives.

Last week, I had the pleasure of going down to Key West to help with a combat-wounded-vet dive challenge. I was the dive master and dive medical technician for them, and I got to work with some of the most awesome people ever. Over half the participants were missing at least one leg, but nothing slows them down. Nothing. Every now and then, I get to do really special events like that.

I also help with Kinetic Adventure Medical Education, run by two Air Force retired aerospace doctors. And I teach jungle and dive medicine for them. I also have helped them out by teaching for the last three years at the Aerospace Medical Association's conference.

This fall, I will teach at a physical therapy conference because one of my buddies is a physical therapist. They're pushing an outdoor theme, so I'm helping him teach a wilderness medical abbreviated course for some physical therapists. I do pretty much anything outdoors.

I currently don't do much community stuff that isn't work related. I actually decided that I needed another graduate degree, so I'm working on an Austere Critical Care graduate degree. It's funny because in August of 2014, I spent a month up in DC at the Department of Defense Traumatic Brain Injury Clinic because I had been blown up. Now, I'm working on the same degree that the professionals had who worked on me.

I find that when I push myself and put myself in learning mode, everything works better in my head. My cognition is better, and my memory is better. I get better sleep when I exercise my brain because it's essentially a muscle. It works better, just like a regular muscle.

My main advice for the reader is to find your passions and use your passion to help others. I think there's too much selfishness in our society today. Maybe it isn't always selfishness, but too many people have blinders on. When everything's more expensive, people must work harder and longer just to get the basic essentials. I think people are so focused on getting up, going to work, coming home, and then running around to keep themselves busy that they don't stop to look around and see who they can help.

10 INNOVATIVE LEADERSHIP STRATEGIES FOR THE MODERN ENTREPRENEUR

In a rapidly changing world where traditional norms and practices are constantly challenged, leadership must evolve. Today's leaders are at the crossroads of technological advancement, social change, and global connectivity. These changes require a departure from traditional leadership models that may have worked well in the past but no longer address the complex realities of our time.

The modern entrepreneur faces a new set of challenges and opportunities that require a different mindset and a different way of leading. As the lines between industries blur and technology disrupts established business models, the call for innovative leadership has never been louder. Innovation is not limited to products or services but also how we lead, manage, and inspire our teams.

Innovation in leadership means embracing new methodologies and technologies and cultivating a mindset of exploring uncharted territories. It means recognizing that diversity, sustainability, collaboration, and adaptability are not only buzzwords but essential components of successful leadership in today's multi-faceted business world.

Today's leaders must be willing to break new ground, challenge the status quo, and venture into new realms of possibility. They must leverage the technological tools at their disposal to increase efficiency and create a more responsive, transparent, and inclusive environment. They must recognize that the workforce of the future values flexibility, autonomy, meaningfulness, and well-being. They must understand that social responsibility is not an afterthought but a fundamental aspect of the modern economy that can drive innovation and growth.

But what does this innovative leadership look like? How can business leaders translate these lofty ideals into actionable strategies tailored to their unique circumstances and challenges?

The following ten strategies for innovative leadership will guide anyone trying to navigate the exciting yet daunting landscape of modern business. These practical strategies reflect the real-world experiences, trials, and successes of leaders who have dared to think differently.

From leveraging artificial intelligence to sustainability, from redefining organizational structures to new methods of engagement, these strategies offer a glimpse into the future of leadership. They show that innovation is not a fleeting trend but a vital, ongoing process that shapes how we lead, work, and impact the world.

These strategies are for the bold, the curious, the compassionate—the leaders who recognize that the future is not just something that happens to us but something we actively shape.

So, without further ado, let's dive into these ten innovative leadership strategies for the modern entrepreneur—a guide to leading with courage, creativity, and conviction in an ever-changing world.

1. **Leveraging AI and machine learning for decision-making**

   Artificial intelligence (AI) and machine learning are revolutionizing how leaders make decisions. These technologies can sift through vast amounts of data and identify patterns and trends that defy human analysis. Using AI, executives can make more informed, strategic

decisions that minimize guesswork and maximize efficiency. AI can also automate routine tasks, allowing leaders to focus on leadership's more complex and creative aspects.

2. Take a remote-first approach

The rise of remote work isn't just a response to the global pandemic but a fundamental shift in how companies operate. A remote-first approach means that remote work isn't an afterthought or a privilege but a standard work practice. This approach allows companies to tap into a global talent pool and promote diversity and inclusion. It also puts results above office hours and encourages flexibility and autonomy, which can lead to higher productivity and employee satisfaction.

3. Gamification of team engagement and productivity

Gamification involves incorporating game-like elements into work processes to make them more interesting and enjoyable. By setting goals, providing rewards, and adding competitive features, gamification can make even mundane tasks exciting. This encourages teamwork, provides a sense of achievement, and increases motivation and productivity. The playful nature of gamification can also foster creativity and innovation, leading to a more vibrant and dynamic work environment.

4. Holacracy and non-hierarchical structures

Holacracy represents a significant departure from traditional hierarchical structures. In a holacratic organization, power is distributed among self-managed teams rather than concentrated at the top. This approach encourages collaboration and empowers all team members to take responsibility for their tasks and duties. It breaks down barriers and silos and promotes agility, flexibility, and a more dynamic response to changes in the business environment.

5. Incorporate the principles of the circular economy

The circular economy goes beyond traditional sustainability practices and focuses on a regenerative approach that reuses, recycles, and restores resources. When leaders incorporate the principles of the circular economy, they can build resilient businesses aligned with global sustainability goals. This approach reduces waste and environmental impact and can lead to new business opportunities and innovations that resonate with an increasingly environmentally conscious customer base.

6. Incorporate virtual reality (VR) into education and training

Virtual reality offers immersive experiences that can revolutionize education and training. Using VR, workers can be placed in real-world scenarios that provide hands-on experience without the associated risks and costs. This technology enables personalized and engaging training programs tailored to individual needs and learning pace. The uses of VR in training are diverse, ranging from soft skills development to technical expertise, and offer a forward-thinking approach to workforce development.

7. Using blockchain for transparency and trust-building

The decentralized nature of blockchain provides transparency and security that can be used to build trust between stakeholders. Whether ensuring supply chain integrity or securing financial transactions, blockchain can minimize fraud and improve accountability. Using blockchain, executives can demonstrate their commitment to transparency and ethical practices, strengthening relationships with partners, customers, and regulators.

8. Introduce real-time feedback and continuous performance appraisals

Traditional annual performance appraisals often do not provide enough timely feedback to support employee development. Moving to real-time feedback and continuous performance appraisals aligns with the fast pace of modern business. This approach provides immediate recognition, correction, and guidance and fosters a culture of continuous learning and growth. It makes feedback an ongoing conversation and promotes trust and understanding between leaders and team members.

9. Create open innovation ecosystems

Open innovation challenges the notion that innovation should be a proprietary, internal process. Leaders can foster innovation on a broader scale by collaborating with customers, partners, and even competitors. This approach taps into diverse ideas, expertise, and perspectives to foster creativity and problem-solving. Open innovation ecosystems can lead to faster development, lower costs, and breakthrough solutions.

10. Investing in social entrepreneurship and social innovation in business

Social entrepreneurship and social innovation in business go beyond traditional corporate social responsibility. They integrate social and environmental goals into core business strategy. By investing in projects addressing social issues, leaders can create shared value that benefits the company and the community. This approach resonates well with consumers, who are increasingly looking for brands that stand for more than profit and combine business success with social impact.

In a world of constant change and complexity, leadership must also change. The innovative strategies described in this article are not trends or fleeting gimmicks but represent a profound shift in how we think about leadership, management, and collaboration. They challenge conventional wisdom, push us to embrace technology, call for a greater focus on people, and demand greater alignment with our shared societal values.

These strategies enable the modern entrepreneur to navigate the turbulent waters of today's business world and become a beacon of innovation, adaptability, and accountability. They pave the way for organizations that are not only successful in the traditional sense but also more resilient, inclusive, ethical, and responsive to the ever-changing needs of our time.

The future of leadership is here, and it is bold, compassionate, and relentlessly inventive. It requires leaders to think outside the box, to build bridges where there have been barriers, and to see opportunities where others see obstacles.

With these innovative strategies, leaders can create organizations that not only survive but thrive, that are not only competitive but leaders that are not only profitable but purposeful. The journey to innovative leadership is challenging, exciting, and essential. It is a journey that invites us all to become architects of a future that reflects our highest aspirations, deepest values, and unwavering commitment to a better world.

Leadership expert John C. Maxwell said, "Change is inevitable. Growth is optional." We can grow, innovate, and lead with vision and courage. Let's embark on this journey with determination and hope because the reward is

already in the destination and the pursuit of excellence, integrity, and impact.

Action Steps

1. Evaluate and integrate technology: Assess your organization's current technology landscape and find areas where innovative technologies such as AI, VR, or blockchain can be integrated. Think of these tools as enhancements and fundamental changes in how you work, make decisions, or collaborate with your team. Consider seeking expert advice or investing in training to ensure you are using these tools effectively.

2. Redefine organizational culture and structure: Think about remote-first, gamification, holacracy, or continuous feedback in your organization. Determine which concepts align with your company's vision and values and initiate changes that foster a more flexible, inclusive, and engaged environment. This may require a comprehensive change management plan and ongoing communication with your team.

3. Align business strategy with social impact: Explore how your business can positively contribute to society by incorporating the principles of the circular economy or social entrepreneurship. Find where your core products, services, or business operations can align with broader social goals. Work with community partners, engage with stakeholders, and measure the impact of these initiatives. This alignment adds value to the community and can improve your brand's reputation and customer loyalty.

BUILD A BRAND THAT RESONATES WITH YOUR TARGET AUDIENCE

In this article, we discuss the importance of understanding your target audience and creating a brand that resonates with them. We go over the different elements of branding, such as logo design, messaging, and visual elements, and explain how they can create an effective brand. We also discuss the importance of customer feedback and how it can help you improve your brand. Finally, we'll give you some tips and tricks on how to create a brand that resonates with your target audience. So let's get started!

Understand your target market

Before you develop a brand that resonates with your target audience, you first need to know who your target audience is. By understanding your target audience, you can create a brand that speaks directly to their needs, values, and preferences. In this section, we'll go over four important areas to consider when understanding your target audience: demographic information, psychographic information, behavioral information, and the importance of knowing your target audience.

A. Demographic Information

Demographic information refers to the statistical data of a population, such as age, gender, income, education, and occupation. This type of information helps you understand the basic characteristics of your target audience, such as their age range and income level. When you consider demographic information, you can tailor your branding to better reach your target audience.

B. Psychographic information

Psychographic information refers to the values, interests, and personality traits of your target audience. This type of information provides insight into what motivates your target audience and what they're interested in. Consider factors such as lifestyle, hobbies, and values when determining the psychographic information of your target audience.

C. Behavioral information

Behavioral information refers to the actions and habits of your target audience. This type of information includes buying behavior, brand loyalty, and how they interact with your brand. By understanding your target audience's behavior, you can create a brand that appeals to their actions and habits, increasing the likelihood that they'll engage with your brand.

D. The importance of knowing your target audience

Knowing your target audience is critical to building a brand that appeals to them. If you don't know exactly who your target audience is, it's difficult to create a brand that speaks directly to their needs and values. When you know your target market intimately, you can make informed decisions about your branding, marketing, and product offerings.

In summary, understanding your target audience is the foundation for building a brand that resonates with them. By considering demographic, psychographic, and behavioral information, you can create a brand that speaks directly to the needs and values of your target audience.

Define your brand

Once you know exactly what your target market is, it's time to define your brand. Defining your brand is about creating a clear and consistent message that speaks directly to your target audience. In this section, we'll go over five key elements to consider when defining your brand: mission statement, values, unique selling proposition (USP), brand personality, and the importance of defining your brand.

A. Mission Statement

A mission statement is a concise statement that defines the purpose of your brand. It should make it clear why your brand exists and what it's trying to accomplish. A strong mission statement forms the foundation of your brand and guides all of your branding and marketing decisions.

B. Values

Values are the beliefs and principles that guide your brand. They should be consistent with the values of your target market and reflect on all your branding and marketing activities. Think about what is most important to your target market and make sure your brand reflects those values.

C. Unique Selling Proposition (USP)

A unique selling proposition sets your brand apart from your competitors. It's the unique aspect of your brand that makes it stand out in the marketplace. Your USP should be clearly defined and communicated to your target audience through your branding and marketing efforts.

D. Brand personality

Brand personality refers to the human-like qualities and characteristics associated with your brand. It should reflect the values and personality of your target market and be reflected in all your branding and marketing efforts. Think about what kind of personality would appeal to your target market and make sure your brand reflects that personality.

E. The importance of brand definition

Defining your brand is critical to building a brand that resonates with your target market. A well-defined brand has a clear and consistent message that speaks directly to your target market. In addition, a well-defined brand makes it easier to make informed decisions about your branding, marketing, and products or services.

Create a strong visual identity

Your visual identity is an important part of building a brand that resonates with your target audience. A strong visual identity helps your brand stand out and be easily recognized by your target audience. In this section, we'll go over four key elements to consider when developing a strong visual identity: logo design, color palette, typography, and the importance of a strong visual identity.

A. Logo Design

A logo is the centerpiece of your visual identity and should be a clear and easily recognizable symbol of your brand. Your logo should reflect your brand's values and personality and be easily recognizable to your target audience. Consider working with a professional graphic designer to create a logo that accurately reflects your brand.

B. Color Palette

The colors you use for your visual identity play a critical role in creating a strong brand. Colors can evoke emotion and should be chosen to reflect your brand's values and personality. Consider a consistent color palette to use across all of your branding and marketing efforts.

C. Typography

Typography is an essential part of your visual identity and should be chosen to reflect your brand's values and personality. Consider using a consistent font across all of your branding and marketing efforts to create a strong and recognizable visual identity.

D. The importance of a strong visual identity

A strong visual identity is critical to building a brand that resonates with your target market. A strong visual identity helps your brand stand out and be easily recognized by your target audience. In addition, a strong visual identity makes it easier to make informed decisions about your branding, marketing, and product offerings.

Develop a consistent brand voice

Your brand voice is the tone and personality your brand uses when communicating with your target audience. A consistent brand voice helps your brand build a strong relationship with your target audience and be easily recognizable. In this section, we'll go over three key elements to consider when developing a consistent brand voice: tone of voice, language, and the importance of a consistent brand voice.

A. Tone of voice

The tone of your brand voice should reflect the values and personality of your brand and appeal to your target audience. Think about what type of tone would appeal to your target audience and make sure your brand voice reflects that tone.

B. Language

The language you use in your brand voice should be simple, clear, and easily understood by your target audience. Consider using a consistent style of language across all of your branding and marketing efforts to create a strong and recognizable brand voice.

C. The importance of a consistent brand voice

A consistent brand voice is critical to building a brand that resonates with your target audience. A consistent brand voice helps your brand build a strong relationship with your target audience and be easily recognizable. Plus, a consistent brand voice makes it easier to make informed decisions about your branding, marketing, and product offerings.

Build a strong online presence

In today's digital age, a strong online presence is critical to building a brand that resonates with your target audience. Your online presence is your brand's window to the world. In this section, we'll go over three key elements to consider when building a strong online presence: website design, social media presence, and the importance of a strong online presence.

A. Website Design

Your website should represent your brand in a clear and easy-to-use manner. Consider working with a professional web designer to create a website that accurately reflects your brand and appeals to your target audience. Your website should also be optimized for search engines so it can be easily found by your target audience.

B. Social media presence

Social media is a powerful tool for building a strong online presence and connecting with your target audience. Consider setting up profiles on the platforms your target audience uses and make sure your brand's voice and visual identity are consistent across all of your social media profiles.

C. The importance of a strong online presence

A strong online presence is critical to building a brand that resonates well with your target audience. Your online presence is often the first place people come into contact with your brand, and it's an important tool for building a strong relationship with your target audience. A strong online presence also makes it easier to reach and engage with your target audience and helps your brand stand out in the crowded digital landscape.

Building a strong online presence is an important step in building a brand that resonates with your target audience. By considering your website design, social media presence, and the importance of a strong online presence, you can create an online presence that accurately reflects your brand and appeals to your target audience.

Interact with your target audience

Interacting with your target audience is crucial to building a brand that resonates with them. Through engagement, you can build a strong relationship with your target audience and understand their needs and preferences. In this section, we'll go over

three key elements to consider when interacting with your target audience: Listening, Providing Value, and the Importance of Engagement.

A. Listen

Listening to your target audience is important to understand their needs and preferences. Use customer feedback surveys, social media listening tools, and other methods to listen to your audience and understand their needs.

B. Provide value

A key element of engagement is to provide value to your target audience. Consider offering promotions, discounts, and other incentives to your target audience to show them you value their business. You can also help your audience understand your products and services with informative content such as blog posts, videos, and infographics.

C. The importance of engagement

Engagement is crucial to building a brand that resonates well with your target audience. Through engagement, you can build a strong relationship with your target audience and understand their needs and preferences. In addition, engagement is a powerful tool for building brand loyalty and customer retention.

Engaging with your target audience is an important step in building a brand that resonates with them. By listening to your audience, providing value, and understanding the importance of engagement, you can build a strong and meaningful relationship with your target audience.

Measure success

To understand what works and what doesn't, it's important to measure the success of your branding efforts. In this section, we'll go over three key elements to consider when measuring the success of your branding efforts: setting goals, tracking metrics, and the importance of measuring success.

A. Set Goals

Before you can measure the success of your branding efforts, you need to set specific and measurable goals. Think about what you

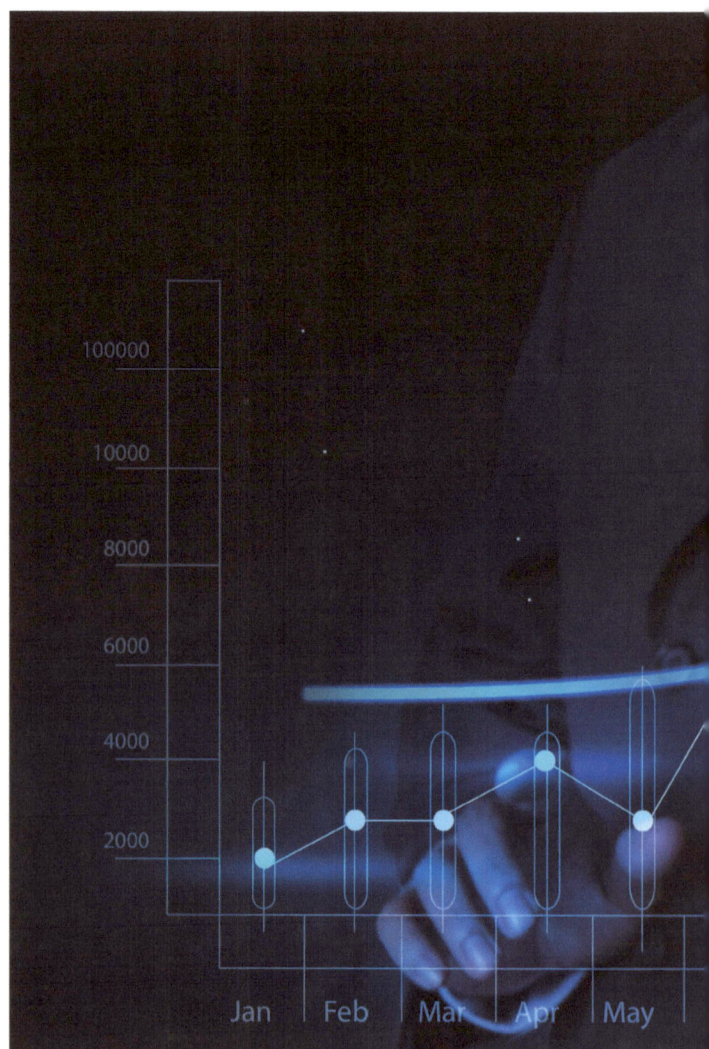

want to accomplish with your branding and set goals that align with those objectives. For example, you could set goals to increase brand awareness, increase traffic to your website, or improve customer satisfaction.

B. Track metrics

Once you've set your goals, you need to track the metrics that will help you measure your progress toward those goals. Use tools like Google Analytics, social media analytics, and customer feedback surveys to track metrics like website visits, social media engagement, and customer satisfaction.

C. The importance of measuring success

Measuring the success of your branding efforts is important to understand what's working and what's not. By tracking metrics and measuring your progress toward achieving your goals, you can make informed decisions about your brand strategy and make changes as needed to improve your results. In addition, measuring success helps you understand the return on your branding efforts and provides valuable insights for future branding efforts.

Measuring the success of your branding efforts is an important step in building a brand that resonates with your target audience. By setting goals, tracking metrics, and understanding the importance of measuring success, you can make informed decisions about your branding strategy and achieve the results you desire.

Building a brand that resonates with your target market requires a comprehensive approach that includes understanding your target market, defining your brand, creating a strong visual identity, developing a consistent brand voice, building a strong online presence, engaging with your target market, and measuring success.

By following these steps, you'll be able to build a brand that resonates with your target audience, builds a strong and meaningful relationship with them, and leads to the results you want. Remember that branding is an ongoing process, and you should always look for ways to improve your brand strategy and make changes as needed to stay ahead of the competition. If you build a brand that appeals to your target market, you'll be well on your way to a thriving business.

DOING GOOD IS
GOOD BUSINESS

SHARING THE CREDIT

Your business can give to charity without writing a check. Visit **www.SharingTheCredit.com** and start giving today.

BUSINESS GROWTH OPPORTUNITIES AND EMERGING TRENDS

The business landscape is constantly evolving and keeping up with the latest trends and growth opportunities can be a challenge for any company. With rapid technological advancements and new business models, it's important to stay ahead of the curve and know what the future holds for businesses. Let's examine the emerging trends and opportunities shaping the future of business and discuss how companies can leverage these developments to drive growth and success.

From the rise of digital transformation and telecommuting to sustainable business practices and the gig economy, we explore the key factors shaping the future of business and what companies can do to stay ahead of the curve. Whether you're an entrepreneur, executive, or just interested in the future of work, read on to learn more about the exciting and rapidly changing corporate landscape.

Emerging trends in the enterprise landscape

The business world is constantly developing, and to be successful, it's important to stay ahead of the curve. In recent years, several important trends and developments have emerged that are shaping the future of business and creating new opportunities for growth. In this section, we take a closer look at some of the key emerging trends in the business landscape and examine their impact on companies and entrepreneurs.

Digital transformation

One of the most important trends in recent years is the rise of digital transformation. The emergence of new technologies such as artificial intelligence, cloud computing, and the Internet of Things is having a profound impact on businesses of all sizes, changing the way they operate and interact with their customers. By embracing these new technologies, companies can streamline their processes, increase efficiency, and gain a competitive advantage.

One of the key drivers of digital transformation is the increasing use of artificial intelligence (AI) and machine learning. AI is changing the way companies interact with their customers, automate processes, and gain insights into their operations. For example, companies can now use AI to analyze large volumes of customer data to gain valuable insights into their customers' behavior and preferences. This can help companies create personalized offers, improve customer service, and increase sales.

Remote work

Another major trend that has emerged in recent years is remote working. The COVID-19 problem sped up this trend as companies adapted to the reality of telecommuting. As companies realize the benefits of telecommuting, such as increased flexibility and cost savings, this trend will likely continue in the coming years.

As telework becomes more prevalent, companies will need to develop new strategies for managing a virtual workforce. This includes investing in technology, such as cloud-based tools that help teams collaborate and communicate effectively. Companies also need to create a culture of trust where employees are encouraged to be productive and engaged, even when working from home.

Sustainable business practices

Another trend gaining momentum is the focus on sustainable business practices. As consumers become increasingly aware of the impact of business on the environment,

there is growing pressure on companies to adopt more sustainable business models. This is leading to an increased focus on reducing waste, using renewable energy, and investing in environmentally friendly technologies.

By adopting sustainable practices, companies not only help protect the environment but also improve their reputation and attract new customers. In addition, companies that focus on sustainability are more likely to succeed in the long run, as consumers increasingly seek environmentally friendly products and services.

The business landscape is always changing, and it is critical to your success to stay ahead of the curve. From digital transformation to telecommuting to sustainable business practices, there are many trends and developments that are shaping the future of business and creating new opportunities for growth. Companies that successfully navigate these changes will be best positioned to succeed in the years ahead.

Opportunities for business growth

As the business world continues to change, there are always new opportunities for growth and success. Companies that are proactive, innovative, and adaptable are best positioned to take advantage of these opportunities and drive growth. Let's take a closer look at some of the key opportunities companies can seize in the coming years.

The gig economy

One of the most important growth opportunities for the coming years is the rise of the gig economy. The gig economy refers to the trend of workers moving away from traditional full-time jobs and instead taking on freelance or contract work. There are several reasons for this, including the rise of technology, the desire for greater flexibility, and the need for affordable healthcare benefits.

For businesses, the rise of the gig economy offers many growth opportunities. For example, companies can leverage the skills and expertise of gig workers to meet temporary or project-based needs without incurring the cost and commitment of a full-time employee. In addition, by working with gig workers, companies can be more agile and flexible, quickly adapting to changes in demand and shifting priorities.

Ecommerce

Another major opportunity for business growth is the rise of ecommerce. The growth of online shopping has been driven by the proliferation of technology and the convenience and accessibility of online shopping. As consumers become more comfortable shopping online, businesses can reach a larger audience and enter new markets.

For businesses, the rise of ecommerce offers several growth opportunities. For example, businesses can sell their products and services directly to consumers through their ecommerce platform or marketplaces such as Amazon and eBay. In addition, businesses can use ecommerce to reach new customers and expand their brand.

Sustainable business practices

As mentioned in the previous section, the focus on sustainable business practices is gaining momentum and represents a major growth opportunity. By adopting sustainable business practices, companies can improve their reputation, attract new customers,

and be more successful in the long run. In addition, companies that invest in sustainability can also tap into new markets, such as the growing demand for environmentally friendly products and services.

There are many opportunities for growth in the business landscape. From the rise of the gig economy and ecommerce to sustainable business practices, companies that are proactive, innovative, and adaptable can take advantage of these opportunities and drive growth. By staying ahead of the curve and embracing change, companies of all sizes can secure a bright future in the years ahead.

Challenges and risks

There are many growth opportunities in the business landscape, but there are also many challenges and risks that companies need to be aware of. Here, we look at some of the key challenges and risks that businesses must overcome to be successful.

Cybersecurity

One of the biggest challenges facing businesses today is cybersecurity. As technology becomes more pervasive, companies are becoming more vulnerable to cyberattacks that can lead to data breaches, financial losses, and reputational damage.

It's important for businesses to proactively protect themselves against cyber threats. This includes investing in robust cybersecurity systems, making employees aware of cyber risks, and developing incident response plans. In addition, companies should carefully monitor their systems for signs of attack and take immediate action when needed.

Regulation

Another challenge for businesses is regulation. With governments around the world playing an increasingly active role in regulating businesses, companies need to be aware of the laws and regulations that apply to their operations. Failure to comply with these regulations can result in fines, legal action, and reputational damage.

It's important for companies to be aware of changes in legislation and to ensure that they comply with all applicable laws and regulations. This includes working with legal and regulatory experts to understand the requirements and develop effective compliance strategies.

Economic uncertainty

Economic uncertainty is another challenge facing businesses today. With ever-changing global economic conditions, companies must be prepared for a range of outcomes and adapt their strategies as needed.

Companies need to have a solid understanding of the economic situation and be prepared for unexpected developments. This includes having contingency plans in place, being aware of market changes, and being ready to adapt quickly to changing conditions.

In summary, while there are many opportunities for growth in the business landscape, there are also many challenges and risks that companies need to be aware of. From cybersecurity and regulation to economic uncertainty, companies must proactively

address these challenges and manage risks. By being aware of the risks and taking a proactive approach to risk management, companies can ensure a successful future for years to come.

The future of business is full of exciting opportunities and challenges, and companies that are ahead of the curve and can adapt to new trends will be best positioned for success. From digital transformation and telecommuting to sustainable business practices and the gig economy, many developments are shaping the business landscape and driving growth.

But it's also important to be aware of the challenges ahead, such as the future of jobs, data privacy and cybersecurity, and regulation and compliance. The key to success in this rapidly changing environment is to be proactive, innovative, and adaptable. By staying on top of the latest trends, staying ahead of the curve, and embracing change, companies of all sizes can take advantage of new opportunities, drive growth, and secure a bright future for years to come.

HOW TO SCALE YOUR BUSINESS, MAXIMIZE PROFITABILITY, AND MAINTAIN QUALITY

Scaling your business is an exciting prospect, but it also comes with several challenges. One of the biggest challenges is maintaining quality while maximizing profitability. As you grow your business and increase revenue, you need to ensure that your business processes are efficient and effective, and that your customers continue to receive the same high-quality products and services they expect.

In this article, we give you tips on how to maximize the profitability of your business without sacrificing quality. We'll show you how to understand your current profit margins, analyze your business processes, invest in technology, optimize your pricing strategy, focus on customer retention, and hire the right people. By implementing these tips, you can ensure that your business grows sustainably while maintaining the quality your customers expect.

Understand your current profit margins

To maximize profitability while maintaining quality, it's important that you know your current profit margins. Profit margin is the amount by which revenue exceeds costs, expressed as a percentage of total revenue. This metric is important for measuring how effectively your business is generating profits from its operations.

To calculate profit margin, you need to know your revenues and expenses. Revenue is the total amount generated by sales, while expenses are the cost of goods sold (COGS), overhead, and any other costs associated with running your business. Once you have these numbers, you can calculate your profit margin using the following formula:

Profit Margin = (Revenue - Expenses) / Revenue x 100

Knowing your profit margin is important because it tells you how much you're making on each sale and helps you make informed decisions about pricing and cutting costs. It'll also help you determine which areas of your business need improvement to increase profitability.

Before you try to grow your business, it's important that you know exactly what your current profit margins are. This will help you set realistic growth goals and identify potential challenges that may arise during the expansion process. For example, if your profit margin is low, it may be difficult to grow your business without sacrificing quality or profitability. On the other hand, if your profit margin is high, you may have more room to invest in growth initiatives without compromising quality.

To improve your profit margin, you may need to reduce expenses or increase revenue. Analyzing your business processes can help you identify areas where you can cut costs or improve efficiency. For example, if your COGS is high, you may need to negotiate better terms with your suppliers or find ways to reduce waste in your production process. If your overhead costs are high, you may need to look for ways to streamline operations or negotiate better terms for rent or utilities.

Ultimately, knowing your current profit margins is important to maximize profitability while maintaining quality. That way, you can make informed decisions about pricing, cost-cutting, and growth initiatives that can help you sustain long-term growth. By regularly reviewing your margins and making adjustments as needed, you can ensure that your business remains competitive and profitable even as you grow your operation.

Analyze your business processes

Analyzing your business processes is important to maximize profitability while maintaining quality. Business processes are a set of tasks and activities necessary to deliver your products or services to customers.

By analyzing these processes, you can identify areas where you can streamline operations, reduce costs, and improve efficiency.

To analyze your business processes, you first document every step of your operation. This includes everything from sales and marketing to production and delivery. Once you have a clear picture of how your business works, you can look for ways to optimize those processes.

One way to optimize your business processes is to look for inefficiencies. These can be anything from bottlenecks in production to unnecessary steps in your sales process. When you identify these inefficiencies, you can streamline operations, reduce costs, and improve efficiency. For example, if you find that your production process is slow because of outdated machinery, investing in new equipment can help you increase production speed and reduce costs in the long run.

Another way to optimize your business processes is to automate repetitive tasks. This can be anything from sending invoices to answering customer inquiries. By automating these tasks, you free up time and resources that can be better spent on higher value activities. For example, if you automate your invoicing process, you can spend more time on sales or product development.

Finally, it's important to regularly review and update your business processes as your company grows and develops. This way, you can ensure that your operations remain efficient and effective even as your business expands. As you grow your business, you may find that certain processes don't work as well as they used to. By regularly reviewing and updating these processes, you can ensure that your operations remain optimized and efficient.

Analyzing your business processes is an important step in maximizing profitability while maintaining quality. By identifying inefficiencies, automating repetitive tasks, and regularly updating your operations, you can streamline your business processes, reduce costs, and improve efficiency. This not only helps you achieve sustainable growth but also ensures that your customers continue to receive high-quality products or services.

Invest in technology

Investing in technology is another important step in maximizing profitability while maintaining quality. Technology can help you automate repetitive tasks, streamline operations, and reduce costs. It can also give you valuable insights into your business operations that help you make informed decisions about pricing, inventory management, and growth initiatives.

One way to invest in technology is to implement a customer relationship management (CRM) system. With a CRM system, you can manage your customer interactions and data, personalize your communications, and better understand your customers' needs. This will allow you to improve customer satisfaction, retention, and loyalty, which can ultimately lead to increased profitability.

Another way to invest in technology is to implement an enterprise resource planning (ERP) system. An ERP system can help you manage your business processes, such as inventory management, production planning and financial management. This way, you can improve efficiency, reduce costs, and increase profitability.

In addition to these systems, there are many other types of technology that can help you optimize your business operations. For example, you could invest in automation tools to streamline repetitive tasks like data entry or order fulfillment. You could also use data analytics tools to help you gain insights

into your business operations and identify areas for improvement.

When you invest in technology, it's important that you choose the right tools for your business needs. This means considering factors such as cost, scalability, and compatibility with your existing systems. It's also important to train and support your employees to ensure they can use the new technology effectively.

Investing in new technology can come at a significant cost, but it can ultimately lead to greater profitability and long-term success. By automating tasks, improving efficiency, and gaining insight into your business operations, you can make informed decisions that maximize profitability while maintaining quality.

Investing in technology is an important step in increasing profitability while maintaining quality. By implementing systems such as CRM and ERP, as well as other tools that streamline operations and provide insight, you can reduce costs, increase efficiency,

and gain a competitive advantage. By carefully selecting the right technology and training and supporting your employees, you can achieve sustainable growth and long-term success.

Optimize your pricing strategy

Optimizing your pricing strategy is another important step to maximize profitability while maintaining quality. Pricing directly affects your revenue and profit margins. Therefore, it's important that you price your products or services to reflect their value while remaining competitive in the marketplace.

One way to optimize your pricing strategy is to conduct market research. This includes analyzing your competitors' prices, understanding your target market, and identifying pricing trends in your industry. Once you know your market, you can set prices that are both competitive and profitable.

Another way to optimize your pricing strategy is value-based pricing. This means that

you set prices based on the perceived value that your product or service has to the customer, rather than just covering your costs and adding a profit margin. When you focus on value, you can justify higher prices and increase profitability.

It's also important to consider the impact of discounts and promotions on your pricing strategy. While discounts and promotions can attract customers and increase sales, they can also reduce profit margins if not used strategically. It's important to carefully analyze the impact of discounts and special offers on your revenue and profit margins and adjust your strategy accordingly.

Besides these tactics, it's important to regularly review and adjust your pricing strategy as your business and the market develop. This will ensure that your prices remain competitive and reflect the value you provide to your customers. By regularly analyzing pricing trends and adjusting your strategy, you can achieve sustainable growth and profitability.

Optimizing your pricing strategy isn't just about maximizing profits. It's also about making sure your prices reflect the value your product or service has to your customers. This helps build trust and loyalty, which can lead to stronger customer retention and long-term success.

Optimizing your pricing strategy is important to maximize profitability while maintaining quality. By conducting market research, considering value-based pricing, analyzing the impact of discounts and promotions, and regularly reviewing and adjusting your strategy, you can set prices that are both competitive and profitable. By ensuring that your prices reflect the value you offer your customers, you can build trust and loyalty, which can lead to long-term success.

Focus on customer loyalty

Focusing on customer retention is another key strategy to maximize profitability while maintaining quality. Keeping existing customers is often more cost-effective than attracting new ones, and loyal customers spend more and refer others to your business.

One way to focus on customer retention is to emphasize customer service. Excellent customer service can help build trust and loyalty, which leads to higher customer retention. This includes responding to customer inquiries, handling issues or complaints promptly, and exceeding your customers' expectations.

Another way to focus on customer retention is to implement a loyalty program. A loyalty program can incentivize customers

to continue doing business with you by offering rewards, discounts, or other perks. This can encourage repeat purchases and increase customer value.

It's also important to regularly solicit feedback from your customers and use it to improve your products and services. By doing so, you show you care about their opinion and strive to provide the best experience possible. It also allows you to identify areas for improvement and make the necessary changes to increase customer satisfaction and loyalty.

In addition to these tactics, it's important to personalize your communications with customers. This includes tailoring your marketing messages and promotions to their interests and preferences, plus using their name and other relevant information in your communication. This way, you create a connection with your customers and make

them feel valued, which increases the likelihood that they'll return to your business.

Finally, it's important to regularly track and analyze customer retention metrics like customer lifetime value and churn rates. That way, you can find out how effective your customer retention strategies are and make adjustments as needed.

Focusing on customer retention is important to maximize profitability while maintaining quality. By prioritizing customer service, implementing a customer loyalty program, soliciting feedback, personalizing communications, and regularly tracking metrics, you can increase customer satisfaction and retention, leading to increased revenue and long-term success. By building strong relationships with your existing customers, you can create a foundation for sustainable growth and profitability.

Hire the right people

Hiring the right people is a critical factor if you want to grow your business without sacrificing quality. The success of your business depends on the people you hire, and the right hiring decisions can lead to higher productivity, better customer service, and ultimately higher profitability.

An important strategy for hiring the right people is to define your company culture and values. This includes determining the traits and skills that are important to success in your organization and creating a mission statement that aligns with your business goals. By defining your company culture and values, you can recruit and hire employees who share your vision and are committed to your success.

Another way to hire the right people is to have a structured hiring process. This includes creating a clear job description, defining the qualifications and experience required for the position, and using a consistent process to evaluate applicants. This will ensure that you hire based on objective criteria and make informed hiring decisions.

It's also important to evaluate candidates not only on their qualifications, but also on whether they fit with your company culture and values. This includes assessing their personality traits, work style and communication skills. Hiring people who are a good fit with your culture and values will help you build a cohesive team that is committed to your success.

In addition, it's important to invest in the training and development of your employees. Not only does this help improve employee skills and productivity, but it also shows that you value their development and growth. This can lead to increased

employee engagement and retention, which can ultimately lead to higher profitability.

Finally, it's important to regularly evaluate employee performance and provide feedback. This will ensure that your employees are meeting your expectations and that they know where they can improve. By providing regular feedback and support, you can help your employees grow and develop, leading to higher productivity and profitability.

Scaling your business is an exciting endeavor, but it requires careful planning and execution so that quality isn't sacrificed while pursuing profitability. By following the tips we've provided, you can increase your chances of success as you expand your operation.

To achieve this goal, it's important to know your profit margins, analyze your business processes, invest in technology, optimize your pricing strategy, focus on customer retention, and hire the right people.

Remember, it's not just about growth, it's about sustainable growth that ensures your business remains profitable and competitive over the long term. By implementing these strategies, you can achieve the best of both worlds—maximizing profitability while maintaining the quality your customers expect and deserve.